REPTILES

Izzi Howell

WINDMILL BOOKS

Published in 2018 by **Windmill Books**, an Imprint of Rosen Publishing
29 East 21st Street, New York, NY 10010

Editor: Izzi Howell
Design: Clare Nicholas
Other illustrations: Stefan Chabluk
Consultant: Kate Ruttle

Picture and illustration credits: Corbis: Paul Souders 12, Bence Mate/Nature Picture Library 20; iStock: CathyKeifer 4bl, astra490 16, FourOaks 18; Shutterstock: Aleksey Stemmer cover, Maciej Wlodarczyk title page and 6, paytai 4 tl, Raffaella Calzoni 4tr, Achimdiver 4br, Gudkov Andrey 5, ShaunWilkinson 7, tharamust 8, defpicture 9l, Rich Carey 9r, Janelle Lugge 10t, Yellowj 10b, Karel Gallas 11, Gumpanat 13, Paul Tessier 14, beltsazar 15, Ery Azmeer 17, Chantelle Bosch 19, Ian Kennedy 21.

Cataloging-in-Publication Data
Names: Howell, Izzi.
Title: Reptiles / Izzi Howell.
Description: New York : Windmill Books, 2017. Series: Fact finders: animals Includes index.
Identifiers: ISBN 9781499483093 (pbk.) ISBN 9781499483048 (library bound) ISBN 9781499482959 (6 pack)
Subjects: LCSH: Reptiles--Juvenile literature.
Classification: LCC QL644.2 H69 2017 DDC 597.9--dc23

Manufactured in China
CPSIA Compliance Information: Batch #BS17WM: For Further Information contact
Rosen Publishing, New York, New York at 1-800-237-9932

FACT FINDER

There is a question for you to answer on each spread in this book. You can check your answers on page 24.

CONTENTS

WHAT IS A REPTILE?

Reptiles are a group of animals that are similar to each other in certain ways. Most reptiles are covered in **scales**, instead of skin or **fur**. Almost all reptiles lay eggs, although a few give birth to live young.

Snakes, alligators, geckos, and turtles are all examples of reptiles.

Pit viper

American alligator

Tokay gecko

Green sea turtle

Reptiles have lived on Earth for over 300 **million** years. Some types of reptiles, such as dinosaurs, have become **extinct**. Other types of reptiles, such as komodo dragons, are still on Earth after millions of years.

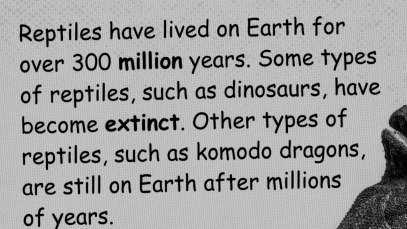

Komodo dragons sometimes fight with each other for food. What do komodo dragons eat?

FACT FINDER

The word dinosaur means "terrible lizard." However, dinosaurs weren't actually lizards! They belonged to two separate groups of reptiles that are now extinct.

HABITATS

Reptiles mostly live in warm **habitats** because they are **cold-blooded**. Cold-blooded animals can't control the temperature of their bodies. To stay warm, they need to be in a hot area. If reptiles get too hot, they move to a cool, shady place.

FACT FINDER

There are reptiles on every **continent**, apart from Antarctica. What do you think is the largest reptile in North America?

Reptiles, such as this agama lizard, lie on hot rocks in the sun when they need to warm up.

Some reptiles, such as crocodiles and terrapins, live on land and in water. They spend most of their time in the water looking for food, but they come onto land to rest and lay eggs.

Yellow-bellied slider terrapins live in rivers and **swamps** across the USA.

BREATHING

All reptiles need to breathe air. When reptiles breathe in, their **lungs** take **oxygen** from the air and help to send it around their bodies.

Blue-crested lizards, and many other reptiles, breathe through holes in their noses called nostrils.

Reptiles that live in water swim to the **surface** to breathe air. While they are swimming underwater, they hold their breath. Some reptiles can hold their breath for several hours underwater.

Crocodiles have nostrils on top of their **snouts**. This means that they can breathe while the rest of their body is underwater.

Sea snakes spend all their time in the water, but they come to the surface to breathe air. Which oceans do sea snakes live in?

FACT FINDER

Crocodiles can't stick their tongues out, but alligators can! A piece of skin connects a crocodile's tongue to the top of its mouth.

SCALES AND SHELLS

Reptiles are covered in hard, dry scales to keep them safe from **predators** and sharp rocks and branches. As they grow, reptiles lose their scales and grow new ones in their place.

The scales on this snake lie on top of each other, like tiles on the roof of a house.

Crocodile and alligator scales lie flat in rows.

Tortoises and turtles have shells on their backs. Their shells are made of bones, covered in a hard smooth material, which is similar to scales. When tortoises and turtles are in danger, they pull their heads and legs back inside their shells.

Every type of tortoise and turtle has a different pattern on its shell. How did this leopard tortoise get its name?

FACT FINDER

Tortoises and turtles can feel when something touches their shell.

DIET

Most reptiles are **carnivores**. They hunt and eat other animals, such as insects, fish, and small **mammals**, for food. Carnivorous reptiles often have large teeth and sharp claws to help them catch their **prey**.

Chameleons quickly **extend** their long sticky tongues to catch insects.

Iguanas spend most of their time high in rainforest trees, where they can find plenty of leaves and flowers to eat.

Some reptiles, such as iguanas, are **herbivores**. They only eat plants. Other reptiles, such as box turtles, are **omnivores**. They eat fish and frogs, as well as leaves and flowers.

FACT FINDER

Snakes don't chew their prey. They swallow their food whole, even if it's very large. Snakes can swallow whole deer, kangaroos, and even cows. How do boa constrictor snakes kill their prey?

YOUNG

Female reptiles lay eggs in nests. Some female reptiles stay with their eggs, and others leave their eggs to hatch on their own.

Female Burmese pythons stay with their eggs until they hatch. They wrap their bodies around their eggs to keep them warm.

When the young are ready to hatch, they break out of their eggs. Many reptiles are born ready to find their own food and **shelter**. Their parents don't look after them.

When loggerhead sea turtles are born, they leave their nests in the sand and go into the ocean to find food. Why is it dangerous for young loggerhead turtles on the sand?

MOVEMENT

Most reptiles walk and run on four legs. Some reptiles, such as lizards and crocodiles, have tails which help them to **balance**. Chameleons can hold onto branches with their tails.

Geckos have sticky feet, which help them to climb tree trunks without falling off.

FACT FINDER

Some lizards lose their tails on purpose when they are in danger. This helps them run away faster and confuse predators. Their tail will grow back later. Which other reptiles can lose their tails?

Snakes don't have any legs. They use their **muscles** and scales to push themselves forward and **slither** across the ground. Their bodies make a wavy shape as they move.

Snakes climb by wrapping themselves around tree branches and pushing themselves forward.

SENSES

Reptiles find out about the world around them using the senses of sight, hearing, smell, taste, and touch. Some reptiles, such as lizards, have a good sense of hearing. Others, such as snakes, sense movement in the ground instead of hearing sound.

A python uses its tongue and nose to smell. Pythons can also taste with their tongue.

Most reptiles have good eyesight. They can see well from far away and recognize different colors. This helps them to find prey and stay away from brightly colored **poisonous** animals.

Chameleons can move their eyes in different directions at the same time.

FACT FINDER

Iguanas and tuataras have a third eye on top of their heads! However, their third eye can't see – it just senses how sunny the weather is. Which country do tuataras come from?

STRANGE REPTILES

Green basilisks live in trees near lakes and rivers in the rainforests of Central America. When a predator is near, basilisks jump into the water and run across the surface to escape.

A green basilisk's long toes and fast speed stop it from sinking into the water.

Galápagos tortoises live for a long time, much longer than humans! Most live for at least 100 years. The oldest Galápagos tortoise was 152 years old, while the oldest human only lived to be 122 years old.

Galápagos tortoises are also the biggest tortoises on Earth. Some weigh as much as 550 pounds (250 kg)—the same weight as an adult pig!

FACT FINDER

Galápagos tortoises can live for a year without eating or drinking! Are Galápagos tortoises carnivores, herbivores, or omnivores?

QUIZ

Try to answer the questions below. Look back through the book to help you. Check your answers on page 24.

1 Reptiles are cold-blooded. True or not true?

a) true

b) not true

2 Which of these reptiles has a shell?

a) crocodile

b) turtle

c) chameleon

3 Which type of animal only eats plants?

a) carnivore

b) herbivore

c) omnivore

4 Most young reptiles hatch from eggs. True or not true?

a) true

b) not true

5 Most reptiles have bad eyesight. True or not true?

a) true

b) not true

6 Where do green basilisks live?

a) in the oceans

b) in the deserts

c) in trees

GLOSSARY

balance to be in a steady position where you will not fall

carnivore an animal that only eats meat

cold-blooded describes an animal whose body temperature depends on the temperature of its surroundings

continent one of the seven main areas of land on Earth, such as Africa

extend to stretch out to full length

extinct describes something that lived on Earth in the past, but does not exist anymore

female an animal that can get pregnant and give birth to young

fur hair that covers some mammals

habitat the area where a plant or an animal lives

herbivore an animal that only eats plants

lung a part of the body that is used for breathing

mammal a type of animal with fur that gives birth to live young

million one thousand thousand (1,000,000)

muscles parts of the body which help animals to move

omnivore an animal that eats plants and meat

oxygen a gas in the air that animals need to breathe to live

poisonous describes something that can hurt or kill you if you eat or touch it

predator an animal that kills and eats other animals

prey an animal that is killed and eaten by other animals

scales small pieces of hard skin that cover the bodies of reptiles and fish

shelter a safe place

slither to move by twisting your body

snout the long nose of an animal

surface the top part of something

swamp an area of very wet land

INDEX

ANSWERS

Pages 4–21

Page 5: Komodo dragons eat other animals, such as water buffalo and deer.

Page 6: The American alligator is the largest reptile in North America.

Page 9: Snakes live in the Indian Ocean and Pacific Ocean.

Page 11: The pattern on a leopard tortoise's shell looks like the pattern of a leopard's fur.

Page 13: Boa constrictors kill their prey by squeezing them.

Page 15: The beach is dangerous for baby sea turtles because it is easy for predators to see and catch them.

Page 16: Geckos and tuataras can lose their tails.

Page 19: Tuataras come from New Zealand.

Page 21: Galápagos tortoises are herbivores.

Quiz answers

1   true

2   b - turtle

3   b- herbivore

4   true

5   not true – most reptiles have good eyesight.

6   c - in trees